Adam

My dear cha
glad I am that someone
has achieved the tender
age of 40 years before me.
But however, I must say
how disappointed that your
handicap is still on a
par with your age.

Yours aye.

Evan & Fhieil.

12/6/1990.

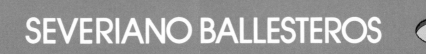

SEVERIANO BALLESTEROS

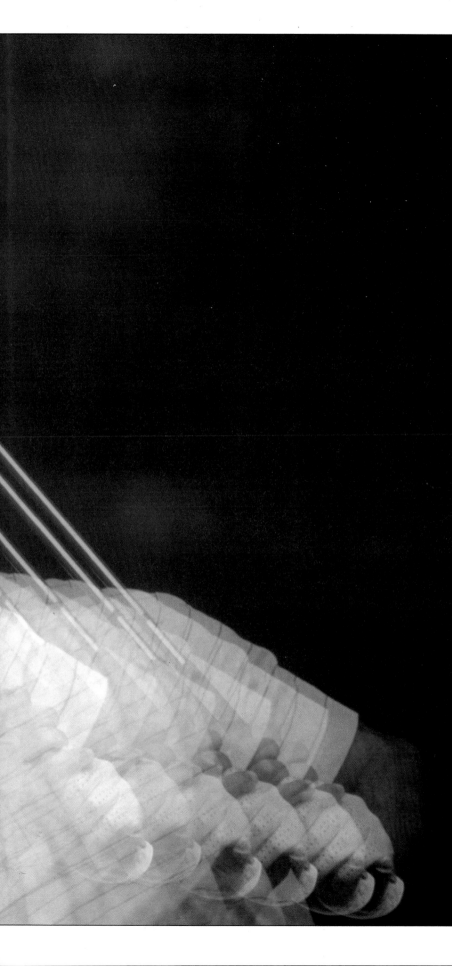

SEVERIANO BALLESTEROS

BY DAVID CANNON

KINGSWOOD PRESS

To Frances
with all my love

The Kingswood Press
an imprint of William Heinemann Ltd.
10 Upper Grosvenor Street, London
W1X 9PA
LONDON MELBOURNE TORONTO
JOHANNESBURG AUCKLAND

First published 1986

ISBN 0 434 98094 3

Designed by Brian
Whitehead
Typeset by Rowland
Phototypesetting
(London) Ltd.
Reproduced by
Mandarin Publishers
Ltd
Printed and bound in
Great Britain by
W.S. Cowell Ltd,
Ipswich and London

SEVERIANO BALLESTEROS

The first time I ever set eyes on Severiano Ballesteros, he was angry. He was 17 and having a bad day when somebody in the crowd spoke as he crouched over a putt. It mattered very little to us because he was just another unpronounceable Spanish name, and I remember thinking what problems the headline writers would face if this obscure young man ever did well.

That day, however, outside Madrid, even though he was of no interest to us as we waited for the newly-crowned US Masters champion Gary Player in the following match, we were struck by the intensity of this teenager's concentration and his impatience at his own imperfections.

It was more than the customary rage a golfer endures when absolutely nothing will go right. Moreover there was a composure and self-assurance that this youth, without achievement or experience, really had no right to possess. He marched towards the distracting voice in a crowd still not versed in the hushed ways of tournament golf and his tone was both stern and paternal as he told the offender: 'You mustn't talk when we play!'

He walked away, unaware that he had just ticked off Pat Ward-Thomas, the distinguished golf correspondent of *The Guardian* news-paper and one of the most knowledge-able, respected and best-known writers of the day. True enough, Pat, now dead, had the kind of voice that carried even when he whispered so it made a good story afterwards that the doyen had been admonished by an unknown youngster. Exit Ballesteros to the next tee and out of our lives, so we thought.

He reappeared several years later between two small mounds beside Royal Birkdale's last green at the climax of the 1976 Open champion-ship and played a most outrageously brave chip shot we all mistook as an ill-conceived fluke. What we did not know then was that we had witnessed the embryonic flourish of a talent that was to dominate the game worldwide for a very long time.

That week, he had strode purposefully to the centre of the stage without any trace of fear. There he was, the son of a Spanish farmer, holding the lead going into the final round of the Open, ahead of a distinguished gathering of superstars that included Johnny Miller, Jack Nicklaus and Raymond Floyd.

Severiano, at that moment, had won nothing of consequence out-side his own country. There was every reason to suppose he was just another victim of that curious phenomenon of a big championship that lifts a moderate player out of his class, until he is over-come by the fear

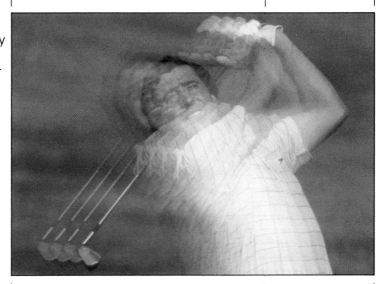

of what he is doing and crashes back to his own level. Accordingly, Severiano carved a suicidal route over the sandhills on that last day and might have fulfilled the archetypal role of bewildered lightweight amongst

the superstars were it not for that extra-ordinary chip shot to the final green and the fact that he played the last six holes in five under par. This young man refused to let go and clearly did not know when he was beaten.

In truth, he did not merely arrive on the scene. He erupted. From anonymity, he finished second in that Open. A week later he won the Dutch Open, then took the Lancome Trophy from Arnold Palmer, and finished top of the Order of Merit having given, in effect, the rest of the European tour a half-season start.

That afternoon at Birkdale, it was possible to detect the complete preoccupation with his own performance, as if the thousands of fans around him and the millions watching on TV were simply looking over his shoulder while he got on with his job. It was that myopic concentration we had first witnessed outside Madrid years before.

The pieces began to fit as we learned more about this fearless Spaniard. He was not, after all, the first good golfer to emerge from the Iberian Peninsula. His own uncle Ramon Sota, a stern, repressive figure, had played in the World Cup. So too had the Miguel brothers, Sebastian and Angel, yet none dominated in the manner of their young fellow countryman, who within ten years came to be acknowledged as unquestionably the best player in the world.

Of course it is possible in retrospect to list the influences that turned him into such a great performer, but for all the time I have known him, I cannot define why it happened. That remains part of the Ballesteros psyche and not even those close to him, not even his closest brother Manuel, really knows what drives him.

Severiano, the youngest of four brothers who lived with their parents within seven iron range of the Royal Pedrena Golf Club on the north coast of Spain, a difficult one-hour drive west of Bilbao, was obliged throughout his early life to keep up with the others. They made few concessions. They were a close-knit group but they were tough. His second eldest brother Vicente once thrashed Severiano, eight years old at the time, for the youngster's habit of crying out to attract parental attention and getting the others into trouble. After the beating it never happened again.

Yet all the brothers have been totally supportive of him, and at times, given up their own jobs – they are all professionals – to travel and caddie for him around the world. But if his competitiveness came from his brothers, then his physique was a legacy from his athletic father, Baldomero. A broad-shouldered and strong-armed giant of a man, he was a local legend of the 'traineras', the rowing boat teams of each village along the coast which raced in the rough, treacherous waters of Santander Bay. It requires not just strength and will-power to race in those giant waves but an unflinching courage that years later, his youngest son was to demonstrate on the great occasions when a different kind of safety had to be ignored for a chance of victory.

One shot surely offers proof of this, when in 1983, Severiano drilled a wood down the hill across the bunker and on to Augusta's second green to demolish the opposition in his final round, and win the US Masters for the second time. For Severiano there was no choice – only a compulsion to attack, break the nerve of others and in so doing prove himself more fearless than they. When he smells victory he strides with the impatience of a man late for an appointment.

I doubt whether there ever was any social ambition behind his desire to succeed. The family were not, after all, poor even if they were locked into the rigid class structure of Spanish society. The brothers played golf, never as members but as caddies, and eventually earned their living from the game as honest retainers. Thus they were addressed by surname only, never pre-fixed by 'Senor'.

His pride, I suspect, was the greatest motivation and when thwarted or offended, made him most determined and competitive. He senses insult where none exists and at times seems to thrive on confrontation as though lifted by its demands, particularly in the United States where he considers himself disliked, and is often the lone figure, idly thumbing through a magazine in an otherwise boisterous locker-room.

Such an attitude led to inevitable conflicts, some of which were hurtful, and all well documented. He commanded huge appearance money and declared he would not play without it. That stance led to his being dropped from the Ryder Cup team for one match. He fought American Tour officials successfully for the right to regard Europe and not just Spain as his home circuit so he could play in more events (and pick up more appearance money). Then he squared up to US officials again and refused to play in the required number of events, and found himself barred for a year during which his injured pride made the winning of a major championship, particularly in the United States, an imperative ambition.

Was this arrogance or a refusal to be straight-jacketed by the rules? This great individualist lives by his own standards wherever they lead him. His results on the fairway have been spectacular and restored artistry to a game that, through sheer volume of financial rewards, had been deadened into a mechanical tee-fairway-green ritual.

He is smitten, if not cursed, by an erratic streak that not only draws upon his miraculous powers of shot-making and escape, but also creates excitement for a devoted public who see him as both fallible and inspired, and regard him consequently as one of sport's top box-office attractions. He remembers the great strokes he has performed and I suspect he savours their memory in his quieter moments. I once saw him play an astonishing wedge shot round trees to the green at Bay Hill in Florida. It mattered little because he did not win the tournament but when I mentioned it years later he, too, remembered the moment.

There have been many others. Indeed it is doubtful whether any golfer, save perhaps Gary Player, the idol of his early years, has produced more obvious match-winners:— the chip shot beside Wentworth's last green against Arnold Palmer in the 1983 World Match Play event; the tee shot to the tenth green at The Belfry that underlined European supremacy in the 1985 Ryder Cup; the unforgettable wood shot from a bunker to the edge of the last green to snatch a half-point in the 1983 Ryder Cup; and the recovery from wide of Royal Lytham's fairway that earned him the unfair nickname of 'parking lot champion', when he took the 1979 Open championship from a very disgruntled and surprised Hale Irwin.

Yet golf has always been more than an arithmetical exercise – a litany of low figures – for this man. When I visited him in Pedrena just after his 1979 triumph he took boyish delight – almost like a show-off – in demonstrating his trick shots, perfected on the course through the endless hours of childhood. The full repertoire was there – the delicate bunker shot with a one-iron, the blindfolded shots, full drives on the knees, even shots through the legs, impressions and juggling acts – evidence of absolute control and an instinctive knowledge of what the ball would do.

What the very great players also possess is a sense of destiny, an awareness that life does have a script and that great victories are inevitable parts of it. It means the good moments can be enjoyed to the full but more importantly the bad moments are more bearable. So Severiano fails to get to the first tee on time for the 1980 US Open and is disqualified? It was never meant to be. He rushes for a plane in Madrid to fly home and misses it by minutes. An hour later the plane crashes. Lucky escape? For Ballesteros, it is 'destino'.

Though not religious, there is nevertheless a mystical depth to his life and its aspects – not a mission exactly, but a meaning and point to his excellence and achievement.

His formidable talent has involved him in a lengthy, sometimes painful, learning process about the duties and pitfalls of being a public figure. He has learned the basic lesson that both he and the media have separate roles to

play and it is a fact of public life that interest does not stop when the last putt drops.

Thus did he learn calmly to answer constant questions all over the world about his painful back, the prospect of marriage to his childhood sweetheart from Pedrena; the rumoured enmity between himself and Bernhard Langer; the arguments with officialdom and the wider political issues confronting globe-trotting sportsmen. He has also been the subject – or rather victim – of the Sunday scandal sheets, with lurid accounts of his love life.

Through all of it he has retained immense dignity. When he moved into his new home at Pedrena, a photographer asked him to spread his arms for a 'look-it's-all-mine' pose. He declined. A newspaper editor thought Severiano resembled Elvis Presley. Would the young star pose in a white suit with a guitar? Would he – hell!

One of his close friends, an elderly Spaniard now living in the United States, once told me: 'He is the kind of son I would like to have. Not because of his achievements or his fame or his fortune, but because of the kind of man he is. He commands respect.'

But Severiano knows that for all the adulation that has made him a top attraction even in TV commercials, his reputation will stand or fall by the record book. Long after we have gone and can no longer testify to his sublime artistry and the manner in which every round was itself a command performance of high quality, it is the statistics that will tell all.

He has set himself a fierce pace. In six years he won four major titles. In the man-to-man combat of the World Match Play championship he has emerged as the dominant figure with four wins in five years. Without doubt there are more titles to be added to the name. That, after all, is destiny. But then Severiano has always been aware of that.

Michael McDonnell

9

Severiano Ballesteros
winner of four major
titles:
1979: British Open,
Royal Lytham
and St. Anne's
1980: U.S. Masters,
Augusta
National Golf
Club
1983: U.S. Masters,
Augusta
National Golf
Club
1984: British Open,
St. Andrews

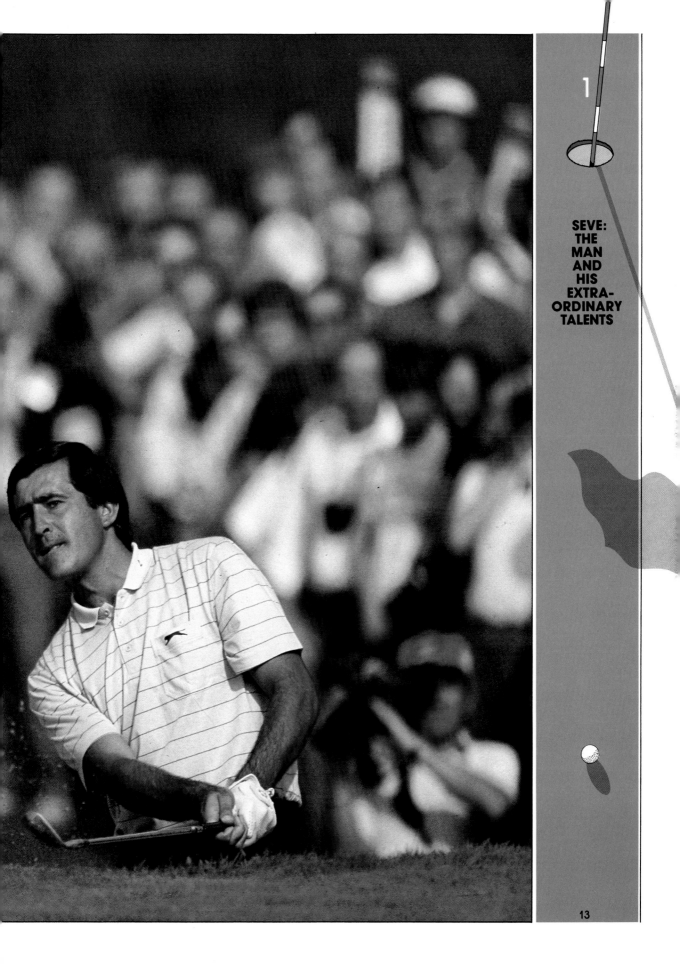

1

SEVE: THE MAN AND HIS EXTRA-ORDINARY TALENTS

Left
Here, Severiano marches over the famous Swilken Bridge on the Old Course at St. Andrews, on his way to victory during the final round of the 1984 British Open.

Previous page
Wherever he plays, there is an electricity in the crowd. They come to watch and admire the power, the beauty and the style of this enigmatic Spaniard.

Initially, it was his fearless ability with the putter that made Seve stand out from even the greatest of golfers, Jack Nicklaus.

Left
Arnold Palmer was the precursor of modern golf.

Right
Seve Ballesteros' approach to the tee-shot is uncannily similar to the great man himself.

18

The swing that burst onto the international golf scene in 1976 still has the youthful power and style in 1985.

From impact to
follow through it
exudes complete
control.

His intuitive feel for
the game means
that he is never
afraid to try the un-
orthodox or the un-
conventional, even
though, just
occasionally, it lands
him in an impossible
situation. However,
his own 'houdini-like'
brand of genius
usually means that
he is not there for
long.

2

SEVE:
THE
GENIUS

Left
Lee Trevino, a close friend of Seve, is another player whose whole-hearted commitment to the spirit of the game can never be doubted, even if sometimes it too lands him in the trees.

Right
Both Jack Nicklaus and Tom Watson use a system known as 'mental indexing' where they picture in their minds the shot they are going to play, even to the extent whereby they can anticipate the ball going into the hole. However, it doesn't always happen just like that. . . .

There is an inevitability that when a new player emerges of such originality as Seve there will be comparisons with those who have gone before. Gary Player was one such golfer. Here, the grit and determination that characterised his career signals another birdie at the 1984 USPGA, where at the age of 49 he finished runner up to Lee Trevino. In all Gary Player won nine Majors from 1961-1978.

SEVE: A PORTRAIT

Sportsmen and women, in general, and golfers, in particular, continually put their reputations on the line. Winning is an exhilarating and exciting experience and it more than makes up for the disappointment and anguish of losing.

All golfers go through bad periods. All golfers ask themselves why the game draws them back like a magnet to the tee.
All golfers seek refuge. Sometimes, one birdie, one perfect fairway shot can release the tension, the pain and the pent-up frustration.... It is part of the drug of the game which makes us want to return again and again and again.

Seve continually
searches for
excellence in his
play and he is more
than fully aware that
the standards he has
set are the standards
his fellow players
seek to emulate.

4

**SEVE:
HIS
EUROPEAN
CHALLENGERS**

At the 1985 Open at Royal St. George's, Sandwich, there were only two players destined to win the championship. They were Severiano Ballesteros and Bernhard Langer. The course was fierce; the weather posed considerable problems. At the end of four long, hard days, neither of the two favourites were there. Instead, the gallery rose to a British champion, Sandy Lyle, the first since Tony Jacklin's triumph at Royal Lytham in 1969.

Left
Ian Woosnam is considered by the pundits as one of Britain's outstanding prospects.

Right
Seve and Bernhard have not only threatened the American hegemony in golf, they now dominate it.

Left
Sam Torrance, the affable Scotsman, who many will remember for his contribution to the famous victory which brought the Ryder Cup back to these shores in September 1985.

Right
Nick Faldo chose to have his worst year in 1985, having promised so much in 1983 and 1984. This year will surely be a watershed for his career.

And even from his own country, there is a Spanish Armada of promising golfers who would dearly like to be as successful.

Left
Jose-Maria Canizares.

Right
Jose Rivero.

Manuel Piñero.

Right
Already Jose-Maria Olazabal has been tipped as the new Ballesteros. He has become the first player in history to win the three major amateur tournaments in Britain; the British Boys in 1984, the British Youths in 1985 and the British Amateur in 1984. Then at the British Open in 1985 at Royal St. George's he capped his short but incredibly successful amateur career by winning the Championship silver medal awarded to the leading amateur who completes all four rounds. Olazabal finished in 27th position on 289, three strokes ahead of Severiano Ballesteros who finished on 292 in 41st position. Already, Seve and Olazabal have had their first professional confrontation in the Spanish Closed Professional Championship at Pedrena, where Seve had to hole a 15 foot birdie putt at the first extra-hole of a sudden-death play off to beat Olazabal.

5

THE
CHALLENGE
IN
AMERICA

Previous page
Augusta National Golf Club.
For many years, European golfers made only sporadic forays into the gruelling, though immensely lucrative American circuit. The best players from Europe seemed almost afraid to risk their reputations across the Atlantic. Severiano Ballesteros has had a love-hate relationship with the American tour and its governing bodies, his main bone of contention being the fact that full members have to play a minimum of 15 full tour events in a year. In 1985 he played only nine and as a result he has been banned from playing in any tour events in America in 1986, though he will still play the Majors. This has proved almost as unpopular with his fellow professionals as with the main television companies and the tournament sponsors. When Ballesteros is around, viewing figures and attendances soar.

Left
Nevertheless, Seve has been immensely successful on the American circuit winning two US masters in 1980 and 1983

Severiano Ballesteros accepts the coveted green jacket from Craig Stadler in 1983.

Previous page
Augusta National
Golf Club.

Left
Nick Faldo, who in
1984 became the first
British player to win in
America since Tony
Jacklin eleven years
before him, reflects
ruefully on his missed
chances at the US
Masters where twice
he had been in close
contention going into
the final round.

Right
1985 may well be the
year that golf
historians will
nominate as the year
that the Europeans
re-established them-
selves in world golf
once-and-for-all.
Seve Ballesteros was
defeated at the 1985
US Masters, not by
another American,
but by his close rival,
Bernhard Langer of
West Germany.

	Palmer	Player
US Open	1960	1965
US PGA	——	1962, 1972
Masters	1958, 1960, 1962, 1964	1961, 1974, 1978
British Open	1961, 1962	1959, 1968, 1974
US Amateur	1954	——

Nicklaus	Trevino	Watson
1962, 1967, 1972, 1980	1968, 1971	1982
1963, 1971, 1973, 1975, 1980	1974, 1984	——
1963, 1965, 1966, 1972, 1975, 1986	——	1977, 1981
1966, 1970, 1978	1971, 1972	1975, 1977, 1980, 1982, 1983
1959, 1961	——	——

The man who was ultimately responsible for the lucrative world of modern golf. His electric personality and exciting golf inspired 'Arnie's Army' of wolf whistling and screeching fans as he charged to eight major victories.

Right
Gary Player

The world's finest sand player who introduced a new determination to succeed into the world of golf. From his diminutive physique he produced enormous strength and skill to accumulate nine major titles.

Jack Nicklaus

The greatest golfer of the modern era who, since bursting on the world of golf by winning the 1962 US Open, has amassed 20 major championship victories (including two US Amateur victories). It is possible that no-one will ever surpass this record, though Ballesteros has the ambition and the will.

Left
Jack Nicklaus

Right
Tom Watson

The most successful golfer of the early 80's, winning six of his eight major titles from 1980 to 1983, including three of his five British Open titles. In the last two years though, Watson has struggled to recapture this magic.

6

THE DEVELOPMENT OF THE COMPLETE BALLESTEROS

Previous page
The tenth green at The Belfry, the scene of the 1985 Ryder Cup and the venue again in 1989.

Left
Seve driving the green at the tenth hole at The Belfry, which is officially called 'the Ballesteros hole'.

Right
Seve using a wood off the second tee during the Open at St. Andrews in 1984, where he won his second Open championship.

From the fairway or the rough his strokes contain all the ingredients of the complete player.

Where the average golfer enters a bunker full of trepidation, Seve enters fearlessly.

On all of the most feared putting surfaces in the world, Seve is at home.

69

7

**SEVE:
HIS
FAMILY
AND
FRIENDS**

Previous page
As a boy, Seve was fond of hitting small rocks with a home made club, which he found on the beach at Pedrena, a tiny village on the northern coast of Spain. When he was eight Manuel, his brother, gave him a three iron. He didn't own his own pair of golf shoes until he was twelve nor a set of clubs until he was sixteen. But, he could bounce a ball a thousand times on the head of that three-iron!

Top left
Ballesteros' father, Baldomero, sits in the crowd with Seve's girlfriend, Carmen Botin. Seve and Carmen are rarely seen together. This is due in part to the fact that Carmen is a student at Brown University on the East coast of America and partly because Seve is very pro-tective about his private life.

Bottom left
Seve and Carmen.

Top right
The Ballesteros brothers; Baldomero Junior, Seve, Manuel and Vicente. His brothers, successful golfers in their own right, have deliberately reduced their own playing commitments to the game in order to assist their brother whenever possible. Frequently, they caddy for him.

Bottom right
Here, Vicente dances in frustration as Seve's putt to win the 1984 world match-play final against Bernhard Langer slips by at the 34th hole. Seve went on to win 2 + 1 at the next hole.

Seve, at home with his trophies and an autographed picture of King Juan Carlos of Spain.

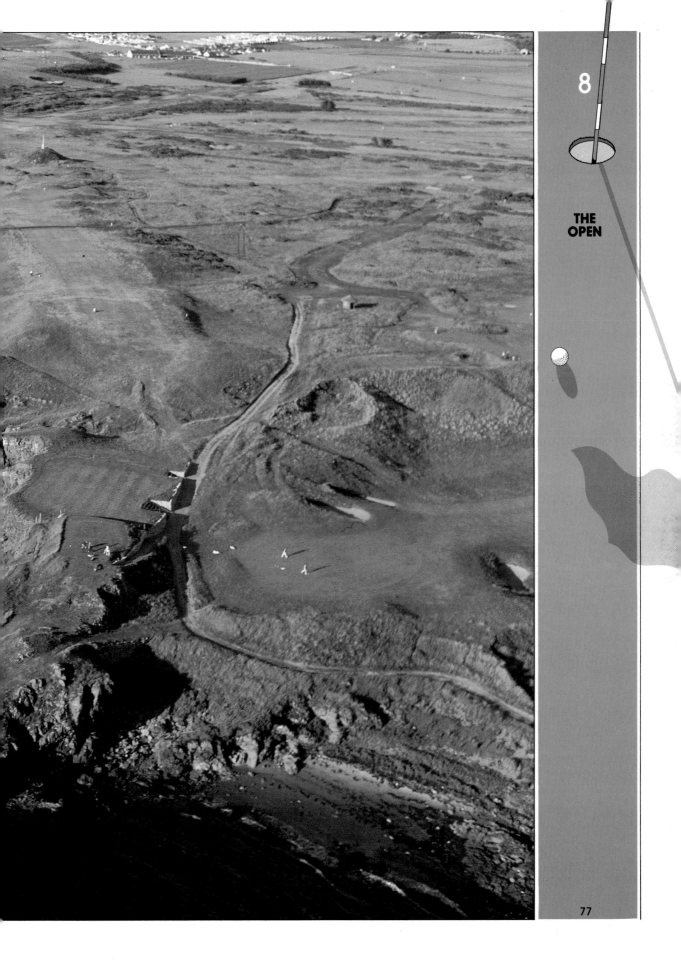

8

THE
OPEN

Previous page
Turnberry, the scene of the 1986 Open.

It was ten years ago that Seve first appeared at the Open. It was a remarkable debut at Royal Birkdale where he finished second to Johnny Miller.

1976: Royal Birkdale, joint second, prize money £5,250.	
1977: Turnberry, joint fifteenth, prize money £1,350.	
1978: St. Andrews, joint seventeenth, prize money £1,600.	
1979: Royal Lytham and St. Anne's, first, prize money £15,000.	
1980: Muirfield, joint nineteenth, prize money £2,000.	
1981: Royal St. George's, Sandwich, 39th, prize money £590.	
1982: Troon, joint thirteenth, prize money £5,400.	
1983: Royal Birkdale, sixth, prize money £12,250.	
1984: St. Andrews, first, prize money £55,000.	
1985: Royal St. George's, Sandwich, forty-first, prize money £2,600.	

It was at the sixteenth tee in the final round at Royal Lytham and St. Anne's that Seve deliberately hit his tee-shot into the car-park because he knew that the rough there would be well trodden. He was also aware that it his ball ended up under a car, as it did, he would be entitled to make a drop. He has always insisted that luck had nothing to do with that particular shot nor with the sand-wedge that he hit from there to the green nor from the green to the hole, where he sunk a twenty foot putt for a birdie, which ultimately sealed his three shot victory over Jack Nicklaus and Ben Crenshaw.

Right
Seve acknowledges the applause of the crowd as he heads up the eighteenth at Royal Lytham and St. Anne's and – overleaf – after sinking his final putt en route to winning his first Open.

Seve's second Open was won at St. Andrews in 1984. His final putt on the eighteenth, which gave him a birdie, is captured brilliantly in these four photographs.

Overleaf
The Royal and
Ancient Clubhouse,
St. Andrews.

Left
1986: Seve will face
further challenges.

Right
Golf is the longest
and most individual
game in the world. A
tournament takes
four days. Winning is
a special blessing as
there are many days
when just one stroke
has caused you to
be listed in the *also
rans.* These four
players will have their
eyes on Ballesteros
wherever he plays as
they search for the
inspiration to
emulate the greatest
golfer of our times.

Top left
Larry Nelson

Top right
Bernhard Langer

Bottom left
Lanny Wadkins

Bottom right
Craig Stadler

9

SEVE
AND
THE
PRETENDERS
TO THE
THRONE

Top left
Calvin Peete, who only started playing golf at the age of 23, and who has further confounded the traditionalists by playing golf with a permanently bent left arm caused by an accident as a child when he fell from a tree.

Top right
Curtis Strange, the leading money winner on the 1985 US tour with an all time record of $542,000 of official prize money in the season. The only other player to earn over $500,000 in a year was Tom Watson in 1981.

Bottom left
Scott Verplank, who won the 1985 Western Open at Butler National, Illinois, where he became the first amateur to have won a USPGA tour event since Gene Litter won the 1954 San Diego Open.

Bottom right
And, the elegant Payne Stewart, second at Royal St. George's in 1985 to our own Sandy Lyle, but always first in elegant attire wherever he plays.

89

Left
Lee Trevino, who
learnt his golf whilst
working as a handy-
man on an El Paso
pitch and putt
course. He went on
with his unorthodox
swing to win 6 major
championships and
many friends for his
outwardly carefree
attitude to the game.
He was a great
influence on the
young Ballesteros,
persuading him to
venture across the
Atlantic to sharpen
his exciting talent.

Right
Manuel Ballesteros is
Seve's elder brother
who has played the
European tour since
1967 and helped
Severiano in his early
days on the tour as
interpreter and
confidant.

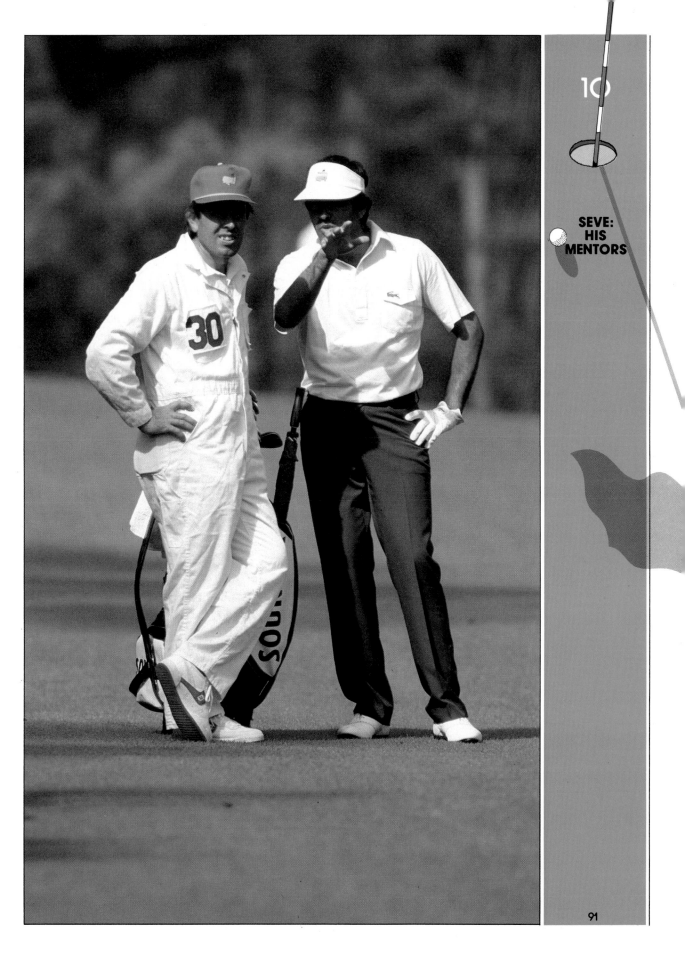

10

**SEVE:
HIS
MENTORS**

Left
Ramon Sota is
Severiano
Ballesteros' uncle, he
was the leading
continental
European golfer of
his era. He also learnt
his golf at Pedrena in
Northern Spain.

Top right
Whenever Ballesteros and Trevino play together 'the hispanic' dialogue can be heard echoing across the fairways.

Bottom right
Roberto De Vicenzo, from Argentina, is universally liked. He will always be remembered for his tragic 'card signing' incident at the 1968 US Masters which denied him a chance of a second major triumph to follow his victory in the 1967 British Open at Hoylake. De Vicenzo was a guiding light to Ballesteros, persuading him to travel the world. More importantly he was perhaps the main influence behind Seve's first major victory in the Open at Royal Lytham. Here he played with Seve during all his practice rounds before the championship.

Seve has different contracts for the same products depending on which part of the world he is playing in.

Seve has a penchant for dark blue. It has something to do with his superstition about colours. A successful golfer today can be nothing more than a walking advertisement for his sponsors. Jorge de Ceballos runs Ballesteros' business empire from Madrid while continuing to work full-time for Iberia airlines as a deputy general manager. Seve's company is called 'Fairway SA' and it is a family affair. Seve owns eighty five percent and his brothers the remaining five percent each. De Ceballos is a director but not a share holder.

97

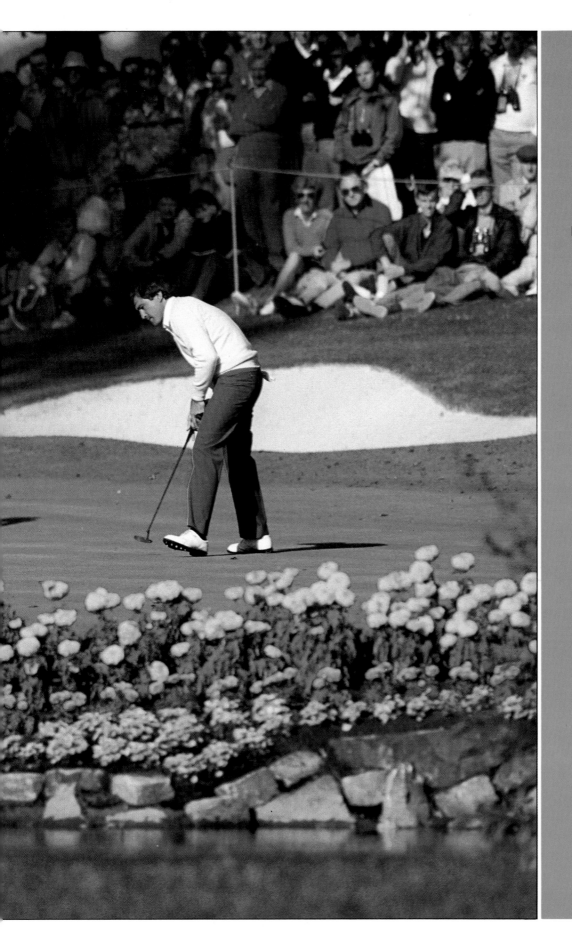

Previous page
Seve and Manuel
Pinero, formed a
magnificent partner-
ship in the 1985 Ryder
Cup, winning 3
points out of 4 in the
two series of four
balls and foursomes.

Seve has been at the
forefront of the
European challenge
in the Ryder Cup
over the last seven
years. His
contribution has
grown from:

1979: 1 point
1983: 3 points out of 5
1985: 3½ points out
    of 5

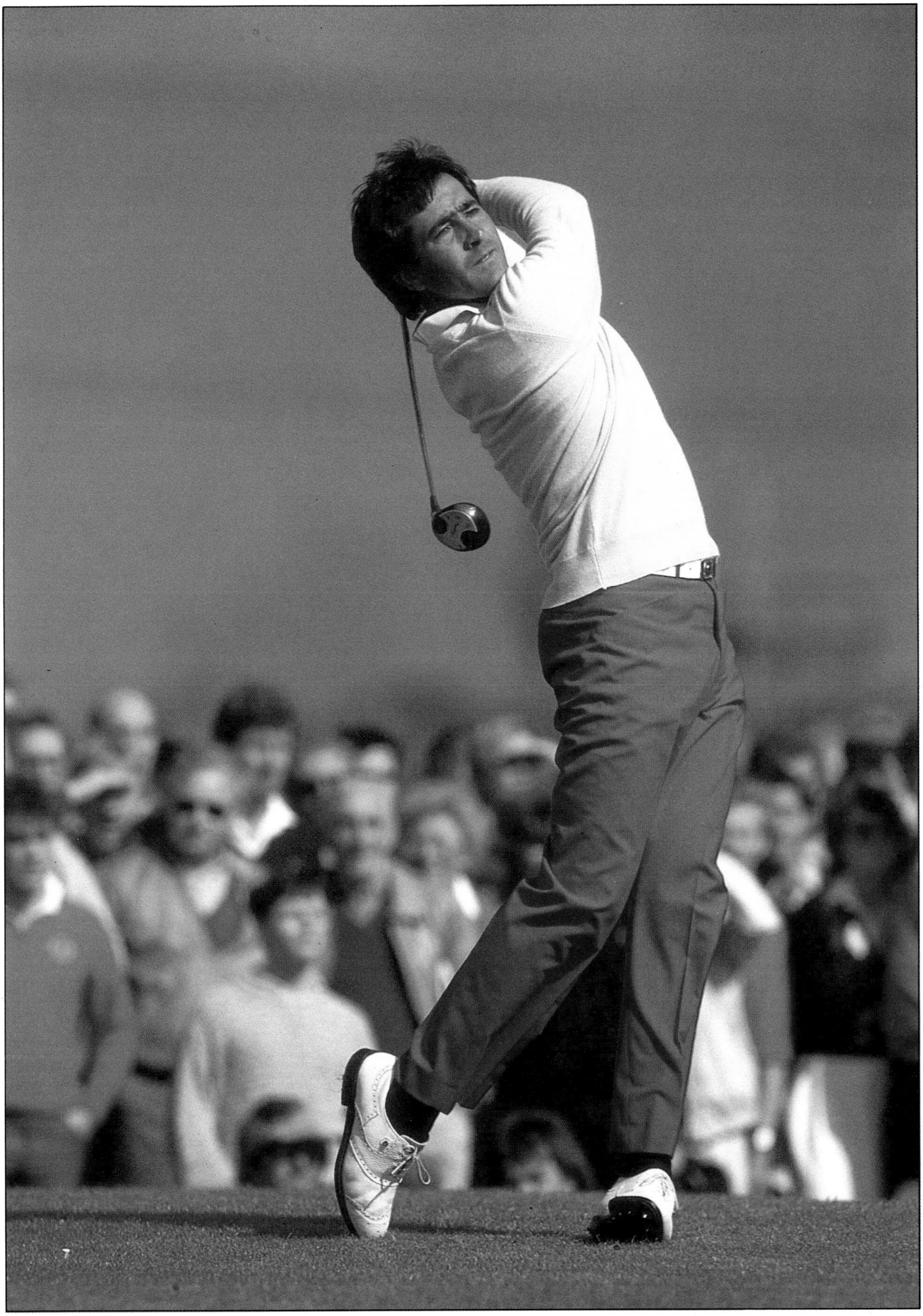

Top left
Tony Jacklin on Sam
Torrance's shoulders
on top of the pro's
shop during the post
match celebrations
at The Belfry.

Bottom left
The four Spaniards
hold the Ryder Cup –
from left to right,
Manuel Pinero, Seve,
Jose Maria
Canizares and Jose
Rivero.

Top right
Team golf is a rare experience in the hectic year of a professional golfer and though there are attempts to create several types of world cup competitions, for the moment, the Ryder Cup is the leading competition in the world and winning it is an extraordinary experience. Here, Seve, the key figure in the deserved victory, soaks his captain, Tony Jacklin, with champagne.

Bottom right
Winning isn't everything; it's the only thing!

**THE
AGONY
AND
THE
ECSTASY**

ACKNOWLEDGEMENTS

I wish to express my heartfelt thanks to all my friends at All-Sport – for all their help and advice.

I owe a debt to my colleagues at Sports Illustrated for their permission to use photographs by Joe McNally (71/72, 74/75) and Steve Powell (79); to Brian Morgan of Golf Photography International for his four photographs (49, 78, 100/2); to Associated Press for the Ballesteros brothers (73); the Liverpool Echo for the 1976 Open photograph (78); and Neville Mariner (Daily Mail) picture of Seve (31).

To my parents, John and Camilla, who helped me through my amateur golfing career. Without their loving support, I wouldn't have seen the daylight and switched to golf photography. Thank you both with all my love.

To Neville Chadwick and John Plant who run Leicester Press Pictures, and whom I pestered mercilessly to take me to Leicester Tigers and Leicester City F.C. matches so I could try out my luck as an amateur sports photographer.

And lastly, thanks to Sue Hadden at William Heinemann for working overtime on the lay-outs, to Brian Whitehead who designed the book and Derek Wyatt, my publisher, who instigated the idea in the first place.

David Cannon
Brighton, 1986